Comics have always been a high-energy source of thrills, fantasy, and fun.

Here is the cover of the classic *Batman* #1 (Spring, 1940), featuring the dynamic duo of Batman and Robin.

COMIC BOOKS

HAROLD SCHECHTER

Running Press • Philadelphia, Pennsylvania

Canadian representatives: General Publishing Co., Ltd., 30 Lesmill Road, Don Mills, Ontario M3B 2T6.

International representatives: Worldwide Media Services, Inc., 115 East Twenty-third Street, New York, New York 10010.

9 8 7 6 5 4 3 2 1
Digit on the right indicates the number of this printing.

Library of Congress Cataloging-in-Publication Number 90–52740

ISBN 0–89471–876–2 (paper)

Edited by Gregory C. Aaron
Cover design by Toby Schmidt
Interior design by E. Michael Epps
Interior illustrations by Karl Heitmueller

Comic book art provided by the Russel B. Nye Popular Culture Collection, Michigan State University Libraries, East Lansing, Michigan. Photography by Amy S. Levinsohn.

Typography: Berkeley Oldstyle by COMMCOR Communications Corporation, Philadelphia, PA.

This book may be ordered by mail from the publisher. Please add $2.50 for postage and handling for each copy.
But try your bookstore first!

Running Press Book Publishers
125 South Twenty-second Street
Philadelphia, Pennsylvania 19103

For Driscoll Reid, Jared Moshe, and Andrew Rubin

My deepest thanks go to Judy Fireman, a steadfast and supportive friend. I was treated graciously by everyone I met at Marvel Comics, and I am especially grateful to Jim Salicrup, Sid Jacobson, Carol Kalish, Gene Durante, Dan Cuddy, and Alison Gill for their kindness and generosity. Thanks also to Ed Dietrich, Tom Varga, and Greg Novak for sharing their collector's expertise with me.

Contents

Introduction

Back in the good old days—the 1950s—enterprising youngsters could earn a little pocket change by setting up orange crates on the sidewalk and selling their used comic books. During that bygone era, it was possible to pick up real rarities for a pittance—classic issues of Action Comics, World's Finest *and* Tales from the Crypt, *reduced from their 10-cent cover price to a penny or two.*

Of course, their condition often left something to be desired. You might well have found a vintage Superman Annual *going for a nickel, but the price would probably have been scrawled across the front cover with a black crayon.*

All that has changed. Today, it would be hard to find anyone who doesn't know that comic books are a valuable commodity. Issues that once sold for pennies now fetch hundreds, even thousands, of dollars. Millions of middle-aged people exclaim at regular intervals, "If only I had saved my collection of *Batman*s!" or "If only my mother hadn't made me throw out my old E.C. horror comics!"

Knowing that something you've bought may increase significantly in value always adds to the pleasure of collecting. But profit isn't the primary reason for collecting comic books.

People love comic books for the same reason they love movies like *Star Wars* and *The Wizard of Oz*—because comics are a high-energy source of thrills, fantasy, and fun. Since their invention in the 1930s, comic books have nourished the dreams of millions of people. Like fairy tales, they transport us to wonderworlds of adventure and enchantment, magical realms of talking animals, mighty heroes, and mythical beings. They appeal to—and help to keep alive—the sense of wonder in all of us.

But if people begin reading comic books out of a simple craving for fantasy and fun, they eventually come to recognize that some comic book creators are more gifted than others and that a number of them are true artists in their chosen field. As comic book readers become more discriminating, they begin to seek out and save the works produced by their favorite writers and illustrators. At this stage, collectors begin to value comic books not simply for their entertainment value, but for their artistic qualities as well.

In the end, people collect comic books for all kinds of reasons, from nostalgia to long-term investment. Mostly, however, collectors are people with a deep and abiding love of comics—their stories, their characters, and their creators.

Whether you're interested in beginning a collection, acquiring a complete, mint-condition set of your favorite series, or learning how to classify and store your finds, this guidebook will provide you with the basic how-to's.

CHAPTER 1

The History of Comic Books

The Yellow Kid

Ever since some prehistoric genius picked up a stick and scratched the likeness of a woolly mammoth into the dirt, human beings have used pictures to send messages and tell stories. For this reason, some historians have traced the origin of comic books all the way back to Ice Age cave paintings. Others find the roots of comics in everything from ancient Roman wall-graffiti to eighteenth-century political cartoons. The ancestors of the comic book were actually newspaper comic strips or "funnies" drawn almost 100 years ago.

The Dawn of Comics

The comic strip is an American invention and was officially born on Sunday, February 16, 1896. On that day, the *New York World* published a drawing by Richard Felton Outcalt that featured a bald, big-eared character called "The Yellow Kid" (because of the

GEE, I FEEL LIKE A BLAMED IDIOT DOIN' THIS NUTTY MAY-POLE DANCE – AN' I'LL MOST LIKELY CATCH TH' GRIPPE FOR MY TROUBLE –

HAROLD GRAY

Little Orphan Annie and Sandy became comic strip favorites in the 1920s.

color of his nightshirt), who would soon become the first comic strip superstar.

Within a few years, dozens of new strips had appeared, including "The Katzenjammer Kids," "Buster Brown," "Mutt and Jeff," "Barney Google," and "Krazy Kat." By the 1930s, the "funnies" had evolved into an enormously popular American art form. For millions of newspaper readers, keeping up with the events of the day was less important than following the latest adventures of their favorite characters: Harold Gray's spunky, frizzy-haired heroine, Little Orphan Annie; Chester Gould's square-jawed crimebuster, Dick Tracy; Milton Caniff's dashing adventurers, Terry and the Pirates; and many more.

The Invention of Comic Books

By the turn of the century, book publishers were already producing black-and-white collections of popular comic strips such as "Buster Brown" and "Little Nemo." These publications did not look anything like comic books, however. A 1911 collection of "Mutt and Jeff" strips, for example, was a long, skinny volume bound in hard, gray covers. Moreover, these early volumes did not contain any original material. They were reprints of strips that had already appeared in the newspapers.

In 1929, George Delacorte of

the Dell Publishing Company hit on the idea of publishing a 24-page newspaper that consisted of nothing but comic strips. He filled it with all new material, called it *The Funnies,* and sold it on newsstands for a dime. This early experiment was not a success. *The Funnies* failed by the next year, probably because people mistook it for an incomplete portion of a regular Sunday paper.

It wasn't until the early 1930s that comic books achieved their present form. The "inventor" of the modern-format comic book was Harry Wildenberg, a sales manager for the Eastern Publishing Company of Waterbury, Connecticut. Under Wildenberg's guidance, Eastern created 64-page color booklets that resembled the kind of comic books we're familiar with today. There were two important differences, however.

First, Wildenberg's contained no original material. They were reprints of popular newspaper "funnies." Second, they were not sold at newsstands or stores – in fact, they were not sold anywhere. They were offered as premiums (like today's breakfast cereal giveaways) by companies like Procter & Gamble, Kinney Shoes, Canada Dry, and Wheatena. People could clip a few coupons from the boxes, mail them off, and receive a free issue of *Funnies on Parade* or *Century of Comics.*

It was left for another Eastern employee, a salesman named M.C. Gaines, to take Wildenberg's idea one step further and, in the process, earn everlasting fame as the founding father of the comic book industry. As in the comics themselves, a light bulb seems to have gone off in Gaines' head as he contemplated the commercial possibilities of Wildenberg's creation. Gaines' brainstorm was brilliant in its simplicity – instead of giving away issues of the new, smaller-sized comic books for free, why not charge a dime for them and sell them at newsstands?

This inspired idea led to the publication, in May, 1934, of *Famous Funnies* #1, a milestone in the history of the comics. *Famous Funnies* became the first standard-size comic book sold at newsstands every month. For this reason, many people regard it as the first "real" comic book, even though it consisted of nothing but newspaper reprints.

Malcolm Wheeler-Nicholson, a former major in the U.S. Cavalry and the founder of National Periodical Publications, was responsible for the next important step in the evolution of comic books. Recognizing that there was a limited supply of newspaper "funnies" available for reprinting, Wheeler-Nicholson recruited artists and writers to produce original material for a comic book called *New Fun*, which he began publishing in 1935. In 1937 Wheeler-Nicholson sold his company to Harry Donenfeld. (Donenfeld changed the company's name to Detective Comics, or DC, and it later became one of the giants of the industry.) But Wheeler-Nicholson's contribution – the use of original art and writing – was the final step in the creation of comic books as we know them today.

For several years, the young comic book industry continued to grow. New titles such as *Tip Top, Popular Comics, King Comics,* and *Wow* appeared on the stands. In late 1936, *Detective Picture Stories* #1 was published. It was the first non-reprint comic book devoted to a single subject. It was followed a few months later by *Western Picture Stories.* By the end of 1937, comic books were doing a solid, if unspectacular, business.

And then, as if from out of the blue, there arrived a figure of heroic dimensions who would lift the fledgling industry on his shoulders and send it soaring.

Action Comics #1 *(June, 1938)*

The Golden Age

They called him Superman. According to legend, he came from the planet Krypton. In reality, he sprang from the imaginations of a pair of teenage science fiction fans from Cleveland named Jerry Siegel and Joe Schuster.

Siegel and Schuster had created Superman in high school and had approached many publishers, but not one was interested. Finally, M.C. Gaines persuaded DC to give Superman a try. The first Superman story appeared in *Action Comics* #1 in the spring of 1938.

"The Man of Steel" was an immediate hit. Within a few months, the circulation of *Action Comics* doubled. More importantly, Superman's arrival heralded the dawn of that era in comic book history known as "the Golden Age."

"The Golden Age" is an important term in the comic collector's vocabulary, and refers to that gloriously creative period when the first great wave of superhero comic books flooded the newsstands of America. Opinions differ as to when the Golden Age finally came to an end. Some experts say 1945, others the early

1950s. But there is no doubt when it began: with Superman's debut in the pages of *Action Comics* #1.

In 1939, Superman was given a comic book of his own, and its circulation quickly grew to almost 1,500,000 copies a month. Inevitably, Superman spawned a legion of imitators. Some of these (most notably Fawcett's Captain Marvel) were eventually knocked out of existence, not by the overpowering might of the Man of Steel, but by lawsuits launched by his publisher. But nothing could stop the superhero boom.

Every month seemed to witness the birth of a new costumed crimefighter, beginning with Bob Kane's Batman, who made his first appearance in *Detective Comics* #27 (May, 1939). Other popular DC superheroes of the day were the Spectre, Green Lantern, the Flash, Hawkman, the Atom, and Wonder Woman.

In November, 1939, the first issue of *Marvel Comics* was released by Timely Publications. Soon, Timely had added its own colorful lineup to the growing roster of comic book superheroes,

Marvel Mystery Comics #24 (*October, 1941*)

followed in short order, including *Animal Comics* (the premiere issue of which introduced Walt Kelly's popular character Pogo), *Looney Tunes and Merry Melodies* (featuring Bugs Bunny, Porky Pig, and Elmer Fudd), *New Funnies* (starring Woody Woodpecker), and many more. Also during this period, America's favorite comic book teenager, Archie, made his debut

Walt Disney's Comics and Stories #1 (*October, 1940*)

including the Sub-Mariner, Captain America, and the Human Torch.

Superhero comics were not the only kind being produced during the Golden Age. The decade of the 1940s was the heyday of other types of comic books, too. The first "funny animal" series, *Walt Disney's Comics and Stories,* began publication in 1940, and over the years featured Mickey Mouse, Donald Duck, Dumbo, and other Disney favorites. Other funny animal titles in *Pep Comics* #22 (December, 1941), along with his friends Betty and Jughead.

Comics such as these flourished through the 1940s, but eventually the public's interest in superheroes declined. The once-mighty horde of costumed crimefighters gradually dwindled. By the end of the decade, only a few superhero titles remained on the stands.

It would be almost another decade before a new heroic age would dawn in the world of comicdom.

The EC Years

There is no universally agreed-on name for the period that stretched from the end of the Golden Age to the start of the comic book renaissance that bloomed during the 1960s, but the term "the EC Years" is as good as any.

Although creative work continued to be done in several genres (romance comics, for example, flourished after World War II), there is no doubt that the comics produced by the EC company were the outstanding achievement of the time.

There is another reason to regard the early-to-mid 1950s as "the EC Years." EC and its creations were at the storm center of a major controversy that raged around comic books during this period—a controversy whose aftereffects can still be felt today.

EC was founded in 1946 by M.C. Gaines. Gaines believed that comics could serve as a learning tool for children. The company initials stood for "Educational Comics," and in addition to the usual funny animal and adventure titles, the company put out a series of "Picture Story" comics on subjects ranging from American history to the Bible.

When Gaines died in a boating accident in 1947, the company passed into the hands of his son, William, who made some dramatic changes. "Educational Comics" became "Entertaining Comics" and began to specialize in a line of brilliantly drawn, imaginatively

Suspense, EC style.
The Crypt of Terror
#17 *(April/May,*
1950)

During the 1950s, a public outcry arose against comic book violence. Some people accused the comics, particularly those specializing in horror and crime, of being a major cause of juvenile delinquency. This anti-comics crusade was led by New York psychiatrist Fredric Wertham, who published a bestselling attack on comics entitled *Seduction of the Innocent* in 1954. That same year, a U.S. Senate subcommittee held hearings on the comics and, in self-defense, the major publishers banded together to create the Comics Code Authority, a censoring agency whose stamp of approval can be seen on comic books to this day.

"The Wertham Crusade" dealt a serious blow to the comic book industry as a whole and to EC in particular. Many companies ceased publishing comics. Others were driven out of business entirely. Within a few years, the number of titles on the newsstands had dropped by nearly half.

EC was forced to abandon its entire line of horror and crime comics. Only the success of *Mad* (which began as a comic in 1952 and switched to a magazine format in 1955) saved the company from extinction.

written crime, suspense, and horror comics. These EC "New Trend" comics, including *Tales from the Crypt, The Vault of Horror, The Haunt of Fear, Weird Fantasy,* and *Crime SuspenStories,* are prized by collectors for the power of their artwork and writing. They are also among the most gruesome works of popular art ever produced in America. Their nightmarish images influenced a whole generation of writers and filmmakers.

"The EC Years" produced some of the most inspired work in the history of comics. But even so, it is generally regarded as a particularly troubled time.

Fortunately, better days were ahead.

The Silver Age

"The Silver Age" refers to the second coming of superheroes that began in the late 1950s and reached a peak during the following decade. It was a period bursting with creative energy, and there was a tremendous surge of interest in comic books among readers and collectors.

Though it is somewhat tricky to pinpoint the exact start of the Silver Age, it is easy to identify the two men most responsible for ushering it in: Julius Schwartz of DC Comics and Stan Lee of Marvel Comics.

Schwartz had been an editor at DC since the 1940s. In 1956, he decided to bring back some of the classic superheroes who had disappeared from print at the end of the Golden Age. He began with a new version of the Flash, who debuted in *Showcase* #4 (October, 1956). In the view of many collectors, *Showcase* #4 signals the true beginning of the Silver Age.

The success of the Flash encouraged Schwartz to reintroduce other Golden Age superheroes. Within a short time, DC

The Flash #123 (*September, 1961*) *featured both the Golden Age and Silver Age versions of the superhero in the famous "Flash of Two Worlds" story.*

The adventurous Fantastic Four were like a family, and even bickered with each other constantly. Fantastic Four #3 (*March, 1962*).

publisher Martin Goodman took notice of DC's success and decided that Marvel should create a superhero team of its own. During the late 1950s, Marvel had been been scraping along on a steady output of monster comics, written by creative director Stan Lee and drawn by artists such as Jack Kirby and Steve Ditko.

In collaboration with Kirby, Lee dreamed up the Fantastic Four, whose first appearance (November, 1961) is a landmark in comic book history. *The Fantastic Four #1* was a tremendous hit, and these characters were soon followed by other offbeat creations—the Incredible Hulk, the Mighty Thor, the Amazing Spider-Man, Dr. Strange, and the Uncanny X-Men.

In many respects, Marvel comics were unlike any of the superhero stories that had come before. Drawn and scripted with tremendous skill and energy, they featured uniquely modern heroes who, for all their extraordinary powers, suffered from very ordinary problems, ranging from financial worries to feelings of personal insecurity. Lee and his collaborators created a comic book renaissance. Characters like "Spidey" and the Hulk became superstars.

was publishing modernized versions of Green Lantern, Hawkman, and the Atom. In 1960, the Flash and Green Lantern teamed with DC stars Aquaman, Superman, Wonder Woman, Batman, and the Martian Manhunter to create a crime-fighting group called the Justice League of America.

Over at the Marvel company (which had gone through several name changes since the 1940s),

Peter Parker's secret life as Spider-Man gets him into trouble in The Amazing Spider-Man *#25 (June, 1965).*

The Marvel phenomenon had another major impact on the world of comics. As Marvel fans began to seek out early issues of their favorite titles, comic collecting became a much more popular – and serious – hobby. Dealers began a booming business in back issues. Fan magazines (or "fanzines") sprang into existence. Comic book conventions – elaborate gatherings of sellers and fans – were organized all over the country, attracting thousands of visitors.

There had always been people who treasured old comic books, of course. But it was during the Silver Age that comic collecting as we know it today really began.

The New Age of Comics

No one can say exactly when the Silver Age ended (though it is usually identified with the decade of the 1960s). What can be said with certainty is that, at present, we are living in a New Age of comic books and comic collecting.

By the early 1980s, hundreds of comic book specialty shops catering to serious readers and collectors had popped up all across America. Within a few years, these shops had replaced newsstands and candy stores as the main outlet for comics. The success of this new "direct market," as it became known in the industry, gave rise to a flood of small independent publishers that produced comic books strictly for sale through these shops.

The first of these new titles was

The Dark Knight Returns #1 *(March, 1986)*

Jack Kirby's *Captain Victory and the Galactic Rangers,* introduced in 1981 by Pacific Comics. Soon after, comic shop racks were overflowing with titles created and distributed by companies such as Eclipse, Comico, First Comics, Dark Horse, and others.

Because these independents sold only to specialty shops, they were not bound by the restrictions

Captain Victory #1 *(November, 1981)*

Concrete #1 (*March, 1987*)

of the Comics Code Authority. As a result, their publications tended to be more unconventional than mainstream comics. Many of these titles, such as Howard Chaykin's *American Flagg!,* Dave Stevens's *The Rocketeer,* and Paul Chadwick's *Concrete* achieved new levels of innovation. As some comics became grown-up in style and content, they began attracting a more mature audience. Comics were no longer just "kid stuff."

Recognizing the growing importance of the specialty shops, DC and Marvel began aiming more and more of their comics at the collector's market. Throughout the 1980s, a crop of young artists and writers produced work of dazzling originality, creating exciting new characters and breathing fresh life into old favorites. Among the outstanding achievements of the decade were Frank Miller's brilliant

The Rocketeer #1
(*June, 1988*)

The Man of Steel #1 (June, 1986)

past few years are John Byrne's six-part Superman "mini-series" *The Man of Steel,* and the twelve-part "maxi-series" *Crisis on Infinite Earths,* in which the entire universe of DC superheroes underwent a major reorganization. Following their initial publication as individual comics, many such series were collected and reissued in the form of hardcover or paperbound books.

Another important development of recent years has been the creation of original works in the same book-length format. These publications are known as "graphic novels." Although some graphic novels are little more than ordinary comics packaged in an expensive form, others have taken the comic book medium in new artistic directions. One of the most striking is *Arkham Asylum* (written by Grant Morrison and illustrated by Dave McKean), a Batman story of such visual and narrative richness that it became the first comic ever offered by the Book-of-the-Month Club!

Comic collecting has also become a more sophisticated matter. Gone are the days when a fan could have realistic hopes of finding a cartonful of Silver Age SpiderMan comics at a neighborhood garage

updating of the Batman legend in *The Dark Knight Returns* and Alan Moore and Dave Gibbons's stunningly original *Watchmen.*

New formats were also introduced. Perhaps the most significant of these was the "limited series" – a comic book title that runs for only a few issues and presents a complete, self-contained story. Two important series of the sale. Everyone knows that certain old comic books have become high-priced collectibles. In one sense, this situation has made collecting harder – or at least more expensive. But the big increase in the number of comic book specialty shops has also meant that it's easier to find sources of old comics than it used to be.

All in all, it's an exciting time to be a comic book collector!

CHAPTER 2

Anatomy of a Comic Book

In the early 1930s, comic strip publishers discovered that a single sheet of newsprint could be folded and trimmed to produce eight individual pages, each measuring about eight inches by eleven inches. Stapled together, several of these cut and folded sheets make a comic book.

The inside pages of a standard comic book are still printed on inexpensive paper. Heavier, higher-quality stock–smooth and slightly glossy–is used for the cover.

In the beginning, most comic books were 64 pages long and cost a dime. Over the years, they became slimmer and slightly smaller. At the same time, they became more expensive. Today's standard comic measures roughly six and three-quarters inches by ten and one-quarter inches, contains 32 pages, and costs one dollar.

Here's a close look at the three main features of a comic book: the cover, the front page, and a typical story page.

Cover

Besides a striking illustration, the typical cover will feature the comic book's specially-designed title or *logo*, its *price, issue number,* and *date of publication,* the publisher's trademark or *imprint* and – in comics published after the mid-1950s – the *Comics Code Authority stamp of approval* (described on page 18).

imprint

price

issue number and date

logo

Comics Code Authority stamp

Front Page

Often, the front page consists of a *splash panel* – a full-page picture designed to grab the reader's interest (or "make a splash"). Running along the bottom of the first page is the *indicia* – a block of small print containing important publishing information, including the issue number, date, the copyright year, the publisher's address, and subscription information. The *credits* list the names of the people who created the issue.

splash panel

credits

indicia

Story Pages

A typical story page is made up of a series of *panels*–small, framed boxes containing the action. In older comics, panels tended to be very regular and symmetrical. Today, the treatment of panels is far more inventive. Panels come in all shapes, sizes, and designs. Some pages dispense with them altogether. Still, the panel remains the basic pictorial unit of the comic book medium. The devices used within the panels include *speech balloons* (which contain dialogue), *thought balloons* (which enclose the thoughts of characters), *sound effects,* and *captions* (which provide narrative information).

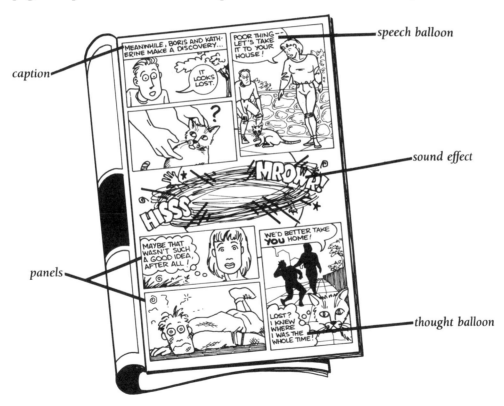

CHAPTER 3

How Comics Are Produced

Turning blank pages into a finished comic book story is a step-by-step process that requires five separate skills–writing, pencilling, inking, lettering, and coloring. In rare cases, two or more of these creative tasks are performed by a single individual. A comic book master might write, illustrate, ink, and even letter his or her own comic books. It is much more common, however, for these jobs to be divided among five individuals, each a specialist in his or her particular area. The entire process is overseen by an editor, who checks the pages at every stage and either approves them or suggests minor corrections.

Writing

First, a writer thinks up a story and puts the action and dialogue into words. Sometimes the writer works with an idea provided by the editor. Many writers prefer to do a "full script," describing the contents of every panel in complete detail. Writers with artistic talent may sketch out their scripts in rough drawings or "storyboards."

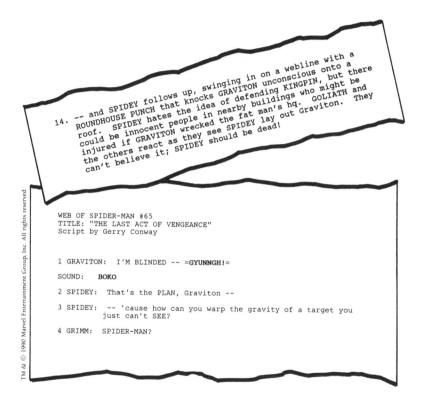

14. -- and SPIDEY follows up, swinging in on a webline with a ROUNDHOUSE PUNCH that knocks GRAVITON unconscious onto a roof. SPIDEY hates the idea of defending KINGPIN, but there could be innocent people in nearby buildings who might be injured if GRAVITON wrecked the fat man's hq. GOLIATH and the others react as they see SPIDEY lay out Graviton. They can't believe it; SPIDEY should be dead!

WEB OF SPIDER-MAN #65
TITLE: "THE LAST ACT OF VENGEANCE"
Script by Gerry Conway

1 GRAVITON: I'M BLINDED -- =**GYUNNGH!**=

SOUND: **BOKO**

2 SPIDEY: That's the PLAN, Graviton --

3 SPIDEY: -- 'cause how can you warp the gravity of a target you
          just can't SEE?

4 GRIMM: SPIDER-MAN?

Pencilling

Next, the script is passed along to the penciller or illustrator, who must turn the writer's story into drawings. Using whatever kind of pencil he or she prefers, the illustrator sketches the artwork directly onto sheets of heavyweight art board, which generally measure 11 inches by 17 inches.

Inking and Lettering

The pencil sketches or "pencils" must then be turned into sharp, black-and-white images that will reproduce clearly during the printing process. This is the job of the inker. Working with brushes, fine-point pens, and India ink, the inker draws directly over the illustrator's pencil sketches in bold strokes and outlines. Finally, the letterer inks in the captions and dialogue.

In another method, the writer provides the penciller with a plot summary instead of a detailed script. When the penciller has completed the pencils, he or she passes the artwork back to the writer, who then scripts the dialogue, sound effects, captions, and so on. This script and the artwork then go to the letterer, who inserts the words into the pencilled panels.

Coloring

Once the inker and letterer are done, the "original artwork" is completed. These are the pages that will be used to produce the comic book. There are two significant differences, however, between the original artwork and the finished product. First, the original artwork is almost twice as big as the final, printed comic book. Second, it is in black-and-white.

To add color, the original art boards are photocopied to 60% of their original size. These reduced photocopies are the same size as standard comic book pages. The colorist then turns these photo-copied sheets into "color guides." Using standard watercolor brushes, the colorist adds dyes to the photocopied sheets and indicates in the margins the code numbers of the various colors for the printer's reference.

Printing

The original artwork plus the color guides are now ready to be used in the production of the finished comic books. This mostly automated process takes place at a printing plant. The printing is done on large rolls of newsprint paper by a method known as letterpress. Once the full-color pages have been printed, they are cut, stapled, and folded into comic books, which are then bundled together and shipped off to newsstands and stores.

CHAPTER 4

Varieties of Comic Books

In one way, all comic books are alike. They are publications that tell stories with pictures. But within this broad definition, there is room for much diversity. From its humble origins as a collection of newspaper strips, the comic book has evolved into a richly varied art form. Here are some of the ways in which collectors distinguish among the different varieties of comic books.

Formats

Comic books now come in various shapes and sizes. There are many different formats available to collectors:

Standard comic books measure six and three-quarters inches by ten inches. They contain 32 color pages, advertisements, and are printed on sheets of inexpensive newsprint stapled together. Some comic books that are sold directly to comic book specialty stores are printed in the so-called "prestige" format. These are similar to standard comic books, but are printed on a higher-quality paper, sometimes contain no advertisements, and are more expensive.

Graphic novels are expensive, book-length comic stories printed on slick, high-quality paper. Some graphic novels have hard covers, while others are paperbacks with square-bound spines.

Comic magazines are larger than standard comic books and look much like other magazines. Comic magazines usually have black-and-white stories inside.

Miniature comics have been published since the 1940s. Although miniatures range in size, they are always smaller than standard comic books. Miniatures often contain reprints, but some feature all-new material. Publishers sometimes produce miniatures as premiums or giveaways.

Hardcover reprints are collections of important comic books that were originally issued separately. Hardcover reprints are a good way to read comics that have become rare or expensive in their original forms.

Genres

As mentioned in Chapter 1, comic books can be classified according to historical period. But people who identify themselves as collectors of "Golden Age funny animals" or "Silver Age superheroes" are not just referring to the era that interests them. They are also describing the *genre* they collect.

The term "genre" refers to a comic book's main theme or subject matter. Here is a summary of the most important comic book genres.

EDUCATIONAL

Comic book pioneer M.C. Gaines was one of the first people to recognize that comics could be used to educate young readers. His company, EC, began by producing uplifting comics such as *Picture Stories from the Bible*. The most famous and long-lived of all educational comics is the *Classics Illustrated* series, originally published by the Gilberton Company, which offers comic book adaptations of literary masterpieces.

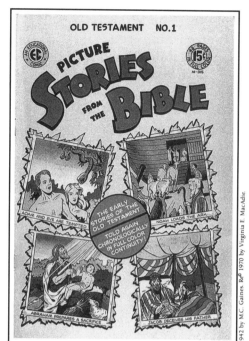

An early educational comic: Picture Stories from the Bible #1 *(Fall, 1942)*

Looney Tunes and Merrie Melodies, feature animated characters. There have also been many funny animal characters created specifically for comic books.

FUNNY ANIMAL

Among collectors, the term "funny animal" refers to humorous comic books featuring animals who talk and act like human beings. The closest equivalent to funny animal comics are animated cartoons starring characters such as Mighty Mouse, Felix the Cat, and Bugs Bunny. In fact, the most popular funny animal comics, such as *Walt Disney's Comics and Stories* and

Looney Tunes and Merrie Melodies #32 *(June, 1944)*

HORROR

Although the first horror comic, *Eerie*, appeared in 1947, it wasn't until the beginning of the 1950s that the genre became truly popular. The best and most famous horror comics were published by EC: *Tales from the Crypt, The Vault of Horror,* and *The Haunt of Fear.* While these titles

Tarzan #22 (*July, 1951*)

had outstanding artwork and well-written stories, most horror comics of the time offered nothing more than page after page of gruesome violence. The creation of the Comics Code Authority in 1954 put an end to most of these titles.

JUNGLE

The granddaddy of this genre is Edgar Rice Burroughs's famous creation, Tarzan of the Apes.

The Haunt of Fear #12 (*March/April, 1952*)

A number of early comics contained reprints of Tarzan newspaper strips. These reprints were so popular that publishers began issuing original jungle comics. Several companies specialized in comics starring "jungle goddesses" who looked beautiful and alluring even while battling alligators and gorillas. The most famous of these was Sheena, Queen of the Jungle. Later titles in this genre include *Jungle Action* and *Jungle Adventures.*

ROMANCE

Full of melodramatic stories about young women who struggle to find true love, romance comics were tremendously popular from the late 1940s through the mid-1950s. The first comic in this genre, *Young Romance,* appeared in 1947 and was an instant success with teenage girls and young women. For the next few years, scores of new titles flooded the market. A much smaller number of romance comics were published during the 1960s and early 1970s. Their readership dwindled, and the genre has virtually disappeared.

SCIENCE FICTION

The earliest science fiction material to appear in comics consisted of reprinted newpaper strips featuring two popular heroes, Buck Rogers and Flash Gordon. In 1940, the Fiction House company launched *Planet Comics,* the first (and, for many years, only) science fiction title offering original material.

Star Trek: The Next Generation #1
(February, 1988)

Science fiction comics really blasted off in the 1950s with the appearance of EC's twin publications *Weird Science* and *Weird Fantasy*. The success of these comics prompted other publishers to enter the field. More recently, popular television shows and movies such as *Star Trek* and *Star Wars* have been the basis of successful science fiction comics.

SUPERHERO

Wonder Man, the Huntress, the Masked Marvel, Phantom Lady, Amazing-Man, Hydroman, Captain Marvel, Starman —the list of comic book superheroes is nearly endless. One expert has estimated that well over one thousand of these incredible characters have been created since 1938. In spite of their great number and variety, super-

heroes tend to be very much alike. Their distinguishing traits include secret identities, colorful costumes, and "powers and abilities far beyond those of mortal men."

WAR

Though most comics in this genre are set during World War II, only

© 1987 DC Comics, Inc.

© 1977 DC Comics, Inc.

two war titles actually appeared during the 1940s—*War Comics* (the first in this genre) and *War Heroes.* It wasn't until the following decade, when EC launched the outstanding war titles *Two-Fisted Tales* and *Frontline Combat* that the genre became popular. These EC publications were so grittily realistic that some critics regard them as *anti*-war comics. Most other titles treated warfare as thrilling, action-packed adventure. More recently, several comics have chronicled the war in Vietnam.

WESTERN

Two titles published in early 1937, *Western Picture Stories* and *Star Ranger,* were the first comics in this genre. During the 1940s, the most successful western titles, such as *Hopalong Cassidy* and *The Lone Ranger,* were based on famous movie cowboys. When comic book readers grew temporarily tired of costumed superheroes in the 1950s, the popularity of western comics surged. With the second coming of the superheroes in the early 1960s, western comics lost a sizable percentage of their audience and have become virtually extinct.

The Lone Ranger
#13 (July, 1949)

Publishers

Another important way of distinguishing comics is by publisher. For decades, the industry has been dominated by two major publishers: Marvel and DC. From the 1930s through the 1950s, there were many others, nearly all of which have disappeared. In the 1980s, many new comic companies were formed. Here, in alphabetical order, are brief descriptions of ten widely-collected comic book publishers.

CENTAUR PUBLISHING

Centaur published nearly two dozen titles during its productive four-year existence. Though poor distribution drove the company out of the comic book business in 1942, Centaur titles such as *Amazing Mystery Funnies, Keen Detective Funnies,* and *Funny Pages* are prized for their outstanding artwork and stories.

DC COMICS, INC.

America's oldest comic book publisher, DC was founded in 1935 and was originally known as National Allied Publications. Over the years, the company's name changed several times – first to Detective Comics (or "DC"), then to National Comic Publications, then to National Periodical Publications, and finally to its present name, DC Comics, Inc.

DC pioneered the superhero comic with its introduction of

© 1940 Centaur Publications

Centaur Publishing's Air Man saves the day in Keen Detective Funnies *#23 (August, 1940).*

Superman in 1938, and its roster of stars includes some of the greatest costumed crimefighters of all time – Batman, Wonder Woman, the Flash, Green Lantern, and many more. It has also published comics in virtually every other genre, from funny animal to war.

DELL PUBLISHING COMPANY

Dell is known for its wholesome, humorous titles. Dell began

From 1939 to 1949, Dell published the cases of comicdom's most famous police detective. Dick Tracy #21 (1941).

© 1939 Dell Publishing Co.

publishing *Walt Disney's Comics and Stories* in 1940 and soon added other animated stars to its line-up, including Bugs Bunny, Porky Pig, Woody Woodpecker, and Popeye. At the end of the decade, other favorites such as Tarzan and Little Lulu were given comics of their own. During the 1950s, when many publishers were forced to cut back or go out of business entirely because of the crackdown on comic book violence, Dell enjoyed enormous success. However, Dell's sales began to decline in the early 1960s and the company left the business in 1973.

EC COMICS

During the early 1950s, EC Comics published a line of "New Trend" titles (including *Tales from the Crypt, The Vault of Horror,* and *Weird Fantasy*), which were distinguished by gripping plots, stunning artwork, and a high level of gore. With the creation of the Comics Code Authority in 1954, EC publisher William Gaines responded with a line of tamer "New Direction" comics, including *Pirate, M.D.,* and *Psychoanalysis*. However, none of these comics was a success. The company may well have gone bankrupt if

Gaines hadn't decided to turn his biggest selling comic book, *Mad*, into a 25-cent magazine, which became a smash hit. EC continues to publish *Mad* today.

FAWCETT PUBLICATIONS

Though Fawett published scores of titles during its 13-year existence, it is best known for Captain Marvel, who debuted in Fawcett's very first comic book, *Whiz Comics* #1 (February, 1940). Thanks to engaging stories and deft artwork, Captain Marvel quickly became the most popular superhero of them all. Because this character bore such a close similarity to Superman, DC sued Fawcett for copyright infringement. In 1953, the case was settled in DC's favor and Fawcett stopped publishing comics.

FICTION HOUSE

Fiction House entered the comic book field in 1938 when it presented the first issue of *Jumbo Comics*, starring the blonde jungle queen Sheena. The main appeal of Fiction House comics stemmed from what comic collectors refer to as "good girl art" – story and cover illustrations featuring beautiful young women dressed in revealing clothes. Because of their provocative artwork, Fiction House titles fell victim to the anti-comics crusade of the mid-1950s and the company went out of business in 1956.

During the 1940s, over a million copies of Fawcett's Whiz Comics *were sold each month.* Whiz Comics #1 *(February, 1940).*

Issues of Fiction House's Planet Comics *are prized by collectors.* Planet Comics #4 *(April, 1940).*

MARVEL COMICS

Like its rival DC, Marvel has gone through various name changes during its long existence. Begun in 1939 by magazine publisher Martin Goodman, the company was originally called Timely. Its very first issue, *Marvel Comics,* introduced the Human Torch and the Sub-Mariner, two of the most popular superheroes of the 1940s. Another major

Richie Rich #4 *(May, 1961).*

HARVEY COMICS

One of the oldest comic book companies in America, Harvey has published titles in virtually every major genre, from superhero to horror to romance. It is best known, however, for its comics aimed at children, such as *Casper the Friendly Ghost* and *Baby Huey.* Other popular stars of Harvey's comics include Little Audrey, Felix the Cat, and Richie Rich, "the Poor Little Rich Boy."

superhero, Captain America, was introduced in March, 1941. When superheroes fell out of favor in the 1950s, Marvel switched to other genres, including crime, horror, war, and westerns. During much of this period, the company was known as Atlas. By the late 1950s, its best-selling titles were a pair of science-fiction comics, *Strange Tales* and *Journey into Mystery*.

The major turning point in Marvel's fortunes occured in 1961, when Stan Lee and Jack Kirby created the Fantastic Four. The tremendous success of these and other "Marvel Age" superheroes such as Spider-Man and the Hulk transformed Marvel into an industry superpower.

MLJ MAGAZINES/ARCHIE COMIC PUBLICATIONS

During the first few years of its existence, MLJ specialized in comics featuring superheroes such as the Fox, the Green Falcon, and the Shield. Although these characters have been forgotten, the company introduced a character who has become a permanent part of our culture: Archie, "America's Top Teen-Ager." After his introduction in 1941, Archie became such a world-famous star that the entire company was re-named after him.

The Riverdale High gang got their start in Archie Comic Publications's Pep Comics.

QUALITY COMICS GROUP

True to its name, Quality published a line of first-rate comics featuring a memorable assortment of heroes, beginning in 1939. The company's first costumed character, Doll Man, possessed the ability to shrink until he was only a few inches high.

Another colorful creation was Plastic Man, a humorous superhero whose body had the consistency of Silly Putty. Quality also published a comic book starring Will Eisner's crimefighter, the Spirit. Quality closed in 1954 and sold its titles to DC.

CHAPTER 5

The Great Creators

For many years, comic books were not taken seriously by most people, including the majority of those who worked on them. Comics were regarded as "kid stuff"—a childish form of entertainment with little or no artistic value. The truth is that most comic books were drawn by "hacks," or mediocre cartoonists who churned out work for a few dollars per page.

Still, there have always been brilliant comic creators with striking, original styles. Comic book fans have been quick to recognize and appreciate the achievements of such people.

Because comic books are primarily a pictorial medium, collectors place emphasis on artwork and illustrators. But comic books are also a narrative form—they tell stories. As a result, there are also a number of writers who occupy a special place in the hearts of comic collectors. Some great comic book creators are renowned as both artists and writers.

Ten of the most highly esteemed comic book creators from the Golden Age to the present are described in this chapter.

Superman foils the bad guys and rescues Lois Lane for the very first time in this sequence by Siegel and Shuster. Action Comics #1 (June, 1938).

© 1938 DC Comics, Inc.

Jerome Siegel and Joe Shuster

Judged strictly in terms of drawing ability, Joe Shuster is certainly not the greatest comic book artist who ever lived. Nor is Jerry Siegel the most brilliant writer. Nevertheless, thanks to a single stroke of genius, they rank above all other comic creators. They are the co-inventors of Superman, the most celebrated figure in comics and an authentic American folk hero.

Siegel and Shuster invented Superman during their student days at Glenville High School in Cleveland. Their collaboration continued after graduation, when they began producing the adventure strips "Dr. Occult" and "Slam Bradley." In 1938, after years of trying, they finally succeeded in interesting a publisher in Superman.

Unfortunately, they signed away all their rights to "the Man of Steel" for $130. Although they never grew rich from their creation, their place in comic book history is secure. Should a comic book Hall of Fame ever be established, Siegel and Shuster will surely be its first inductees.

A pivotal moment in the life of Bob Kane's Batman. Detective Comics #33 *(November, 1939).*

Bob Kane

Like Siegel and Shuster, Bob Kane entered the comic book business right out of high school. His earliest work consisted of humorous features such as "Peter Pupp" and "Gumshoe Gus."

One Friday afternoon in 1939, Kane's editor at DC Comics suggested that the young cartoonist try his hand at creating a superhero character. Over the weekend, Kane came up with the basic concept for a new costumed crimefighter. Writer Bill Finger, Kane's friend and collaborator, made important modifications to Kane's original design. By Monday morning, the pair had created the figure who would become the second most famous and durable of all superheroes: Batman.

Until the mid-1960s, Kane's signature appeared prominently on every Batman feature published, though much of the writing and drawing was done by his assistants, particularly Finger and artist Jerry Robinson. Still, there is no doubt that Kane not only came up with the original idea for Batman but also established the comic's dark, dramatic, and compelling style.

Will Eisner

Will Eisner was barely out of his teens when, in 1937, he co-founded a studio where comic book artists turned out material for various publishers. Eisner himself wrote and drew an assortment of features, including the detective strip "Muss 'em Up Donovan" and a pirate adventure entitled "Hawks of the Seas." He is also credited with creating such popular characters as Blackhawk and Sheena, Queen of the Jungle.

His most celebrated creation is *The Spirit,* a comic book first produced in 1940 as a weekly newspaper insert. The Spirit was a highly unusual comic book hero. Unlike other costumed crime-fighters who dressed like circus acrobats, he wore a baggy business suit and a tiny mask that barely covered his eyes.

More importantly, the plots, characterization, and artwork of Eisner's stories were unusually rich and complex. Eisner's experiments with composition and form opened up new possibilities of visual storytelling for comic book artists and showed that comic books could be as visually interesting as the most exciting movies. Fans and professionals alike consider Will Eisner to be one of the field's true creative geniuses.

Will Eisner uses lighting to create a mood of mystery in these panels from The Spirit *(September 19, 1948).*

Carl Barks

Carl Barks's name, like Will Eisner's, invariably appears near the very top of the list whenever comic book fans are asked to rank the greatest creators of all time. For his entire professional life, however, his name was completely unknown. To his many admirers, he was simply known as "the Good Artist."

Barks is one of the few comic book greats who is associated with funny animal comics and not superheroes. For more than 20 years, he wrote, pencilled, and inked hundreds of Donald Duck stories that are now recognized as comic book classics.

Barks began his cartooning career in 1935 as an animator for the Walt Disney studio. After a few months, he was transferred to the story department, where he sketched gag ideas for comic strips

Donald Duck prepares for a day at work, courtesy of Carl Barks. From Walt Disney's Comics and Stories #264 (October, 1962).

and cartoons. When he left the studio seven years later, he was hired by Dell Publishing Company to produce Donald Duck features for *Walt Disney's Comics and Stories*. His work, done anonymously like that of all Disney employees, proved tremendously popular with readers. One of his greatest achievements was the creation of Uncle Scrooge McDuck, who first appeared in 1947.

By the time Barks retired in 1965, his devoted fans had finally discovered his identity. Since then, his fame among collectors has grown every year. His collected works have been reprinted in expensive, boxed volumes, and his original oil paintings of Disney characters sell for thousands of dollars.

Jack Kirby

Jack Kirby is the only Golden Age great who went on to become a major figure during the Silver Age. In fact, without Kirby there might not have *been* a Silver Age.

After a brief stint as a cartoon animator, Kirby began drawing newspaper comic strips in 1936. He broke into comic books in 1938 and, a few years later, began a celebrated partnership with artist/writer Joe Simon. Together, they created one of the most famous Golden Age superheroes, Captain America. While Simon clearly made significant contributions, it was Kirby who did the lion's share of the actual artwork and writing.

The Silver Surfer, one of Jack Kirby's many famous creations. From The Fantastic Four *#77 (August, 1968).*

Like Will Eisner, Kirby permanently changed the look of the comics. Among his many contributions is the full-page splash panel. Kirby is also the acknowledged master of slam-bang comic book action.

Kirby and Simon split up in 1956. A few years later, Kirby joined the Marvel Comics Group where, in collaboration with writer/editor Stan Lee, he invented the Fantastic Four, the Hulk, Thor, and the Avengers – the characters that transformed Marvel into the industry leader.

In the early 1970s, Kirby parted company with Lee and moved to DC Comics, where he continued to produce brilliant comics such as *The New Gods* and *Forever People.* To collectors and fans, Kirby is known as "the king of comic books."

Frank Frazetta

While Eisner and Kirby have been creating comic books for decades, Frank Frazetta spent only a relatively brief period as a comic book illustrator. During that time, however, he won a reputation as one of the best artists to ever work in the field.

Frazetta's first comic book work appeared in 1944. For the next several years, he turned out a large variety of features, from funny animal stories to a hillbilly strip called "Louie Lazybones." By the beginning of the 1950s, he was specializing in beautifully drawn action comics featuring dramatic

Trouble in the jungle from Frank Frazetta's Thun'da *#1 (1952).*

heroes. His greatest achievement of this period was a Tarzan-inspired jungle comic called *Thun'da,* published in 1952. During the same period, Frazetta also created popular romance stories and superb cover and story art for EC horror titles.

After a stint pencilling newspaper comic strips, Frazetta became a freelance artist, producing dynamic illustrations for books, calendars, posters, and magazines. His stunning paintings for the *Conan the Barbarian* paperback books of the 1960s helped turn that character into a popular figure.

Harvey Kurtzman

As a writer, editor, and artist, Harvey Kurtzman has had a major impact on American comic books, even though, like Frank Frazetta, he worked within the industry for only ten years or so.

Kurtzman entered the business in 1943 and spent most of the decade working on both action and humor features for various publications. His most notable creation during this period was a one-page gag strip called "Hey Look," which featured Kurtzman's unique brand of off-the-wall humor and wildly inventive cartooning.

Kurtzman joined EC in 1950, where he worked on two very different kinds of comic books. He began by producing a pair of war titles, *Two-Fisted Tales* and *Frontline*

Harvey Kurtzman is known for his visual jokes, like this one from Mad #6 *(August/September, 1953).*

Combat, which introduced a new dimension of grim realism into comics. Then, in 1952, he was instrumental in creating *Mad,* the first 24 issues of which were published in standard comic book format and owe much of their brilliance to Kurtzman's comedic genius.

In 1955, *Mad* switched from comic book form to a black-and-white magazine format, and Kurtzman left EC. Later, he produced comic strips for magazines. The work he did between 1945 and 1955, and particularly during his years at EC, remains a high point in the history of American comic books.

Alan Moore

Many fans and critics consider Alan Moore the most brilliantly original comic book creator to come along in years. What makes Moore's high standing among fans unusual is that, unlike most comic book superstars, he is a writer and not an illustrator.

A resident of Northampton, England, Moore first gained a reputation in the comic book world as a writer for the British science fiction comic magazine *2000 A.D.* His American debut came in 1983, when he began scripting the DC horror comic *Saga of the Swamp Thing.* Moore's thought-provoking, geniunely disturbing stories, illustrated by Steve Bissette and John Totleben,

Dr. Manhattan, one of Alan Moore's most intriguing characters, contemplates the cosmos in Watchmen #4 *(December, 1986).*

breathed new life into a tired character and turned the title into a huge hit.

To date, however, Moore's most impressive achievement has been a comic book epic for adults called *Watchmen*. It is the violent and complex story of a group of aging superheroes and how the world responds to them. Drawn by Dave Gibbons, *Watchmen* is as involving as many novels. More than any other contemporary creator, Moore has shown that comic books can approach the sophistication of literature.

Frank Miller

As a writer and illustrator, Frank Miller has had a major impact on the contemporary comic book scene.

Miller was only twenty years old when he became a professional comic book artist in 1977. Two years later, he began drawing *Daredevil* for Marvel. His exciting, cinematic style won him a growing number of fans. Two years later, he took over the writing chores as well. His reputation soared, as did the sales of *Daredevil,* which suddenly became a top-selling title.

During the next few years, Miller wrote and pencilled *Ronin,* a highly imaginative science-fiction action series for DC, and wrote an impressive string of works for Marvel, including a Daredevil

Dizzying action abounds in Frank Miller's **Batman: The Dark Knight Returns #1** *(March, 1986).*

graphic novel and an eight-issue series called *Electra: Assassin* (both drawn by Bill Sienkiewicz).

His masterpiece to date is the mini-series *Batman: The Dark Knight Returns,* published by DC in 1986. This work envisioned the familiar figure of the Caped Crusader as an obsessive man haunted by the ghosts of his past. Miller's Batman was an epic hero for the 1980s and served as a major inspiration for the *Batman* movie of 1989. Miller's dynamic technique as a graphic storyteller has made him one of the most influential creators of his generation.

Other Great Comic Book Artists

Besides the comic book greats described above, there are a number of artists whose work is highly valued by collectors. The following alphabetical list includes many of the major names in the field of comic book art, plus a few of the issues containing their work.

Neal Adams (*Deadman* #1–7; *Green Lantern* #76–89)

C.C. Beck (*Whiz* #1–22)

Brian Bolland (*Camelot 3000; Batman: The Killing Joke*)

John Buscema (*Avengers* #41–66; *Conan* #93–126)

John Byrne (*X-Men* #111–143; *Fantastic Four* #269–293; *The Man of Steel* #1–6)

Howard Chaykin (*American Flagg!* #1–12)

Gene Colan (*Daredevil* #20–49; *Howard the Duck* #4–15)

Jack Cole (*Smash* #18–38)

Jack Davis (*Tales from the Crypt* #24–46; *Rawhide Kid* #33–35)

Steve Ditko (*Amazing Spider-Man* #1–38; *Beware the Creeper* #1–5)

Will Elder (*Mad* #1–24)

Bill Everett (*Marvel Mystery* #1–28; *Heroic* #1–9)

Lou Fine (*Smash* #14–22; *Wonderworld* #3–11)

Mike Grell (*Jon Sable, Freelance* #1–43; *Green Arrow: The Long Bow Hunters*)

Mike Kaluta (*The Shadow* #1–4; *Starstruck* #1–6)

Gil Kane (*Green Lantern* #1–61; *Sword of the Atom* #1–4)

Joe Kubert (*Our Army at War* #83–170; *The Brave and the Bold* #1–24)

Russ Manning (*Tarzan* #39–126)

Todd McFarlane (*Amazing Spider-Man* #298–328; *Incredible Hulk* #330–346)

George Perez (*New Teen Titans* #1–40; *Crisis on Infinite Earths* #1–12; *Avengers* #198–202)

John Severin (*Two-Fisted Tales* #34–41; *Kull the Conqueror* #2–9)

Bill Sienkiewicz (*Moon Knight* #1–15; *New Mutants* #18–31)

Jim Steranko (*Strange Tales* #151–163; *Nick Fury, Agent of S.H.I.E.L.D.* #1–2)

Barry Windsor-Smith (*Conan the Barbarian* #1–16)

Wally Wood (*Weird Science Fantasy* #23–29; *Mad* #1–24)

Bernie Wrightson (*Swamp Thing* #1–10; *House of Mystery* #193–195)

CHAPTER 6

Getting Started

In the old days, comic collecting was a very simple matter. You walked to the corner candy store, forked over a dime for the latest issue of your favorite comic, carried it home, and then (after spending an enjoyable hour or so reading it) stuck it on a shelf with all your other comic books, where it gathered dust and drove your mother crazy.

Things are different today.

Corner candy stores have become scarce and comic books cost ten times what they used to.

Some comic book collectors have become so serious about their hobby that they refer to themselves as "panelologists."

But even serious collectors are people who started out by reading comic books strictly for enjoyment. Most people begin their collections by buying, reading, and saving current issues, and then moving on to specialization and the acquisition of harder-to-find (and more expensive) back issues.

Learning What You Like

Most beginning collectors don't realize the large and exciting range of comic books available today. Some companies produce 50 titles every month!

Because there is so much to choose from, the first step of the collecting process should consist of a period of exploration and discovery. The beginning collector needs time to find out what comics are being published, sample a variety of them, and decide which ones he or she enjoys the most.

To do this, you must first find a nearby outlet for comic books. Sometimes a local magazine or convenience store will offer a healthy selection. Your best bet, however, is a comic book specialty shop. To find out if there is one near you, check your local telephone

directory under "Comic Books," "Collectibles," or "Book Dealers— New and Used."

Once you've found a source for current comic books, sample the ones that seem most interesting to you. Take some time to look over the racks. Pick out a few issues and flip through their pages. (Always handle a comic book with care.) Shop owners don't like to have their stores used as libraries, but most permit a reasonable amount of browsing.

If you're buying comics at a speciality store, ask for recommendations. Talk to the owner, the employees, or other customers. Find out which titles are current bestsellers, which ones feature work by outstanding artists, and which contain exciting characters and imaginative stories.

For the next few months, you should try to sample many different comics. At this stage, you should stick strictly to new comic books. You'll be buying them for their cover price, so they won't drain your financial resources. If you're interested in reading something older, such as a Silver Age superhero comic, look for an inexpensive reprint.

Another important rule for the beginning collector is this: buy only those comics you think you'll enjoy, without worrying about their possible worth in the future. Beginners should never buy a comic book because they think (or some "expert" tells them) that it is bound to increase in value. With new comic books, most financial predictions are totally unreliable.

Your choices should be based on your own likes and dislikes.

Once you've spent some time familiarizing yourself with the current comic book scene, you'll discover your preferences. Certain comics will excite your imagination and fill you with pleasure. At this point, you'll have a solid idea about which comics you want to collect. There are no set rules except one: collect what makes you happy!

Building Your Collection

Once you know what you like, you can specialize in those comics that you care most deeply about.

The ultimate goal of many collectors is to put together a "complete set." This means owning every issue of a particular title, beginning with Number One. Of course, the difficulty and cost of acquiring a complete set depends on which title you choose to collect. It is easier and less expensive to assemble a complete set of *Teenage Mutant Ninja Turtles* (which began publication in 1984) than to collect a complete set of *The Amazing Spider-Man,* the first

issue of which sells for several thousand dollars in mint condition.

Collecting comics by title is the most common approach. There are also ways of collecting that combine several approaches. Here are a few of the most popular ones:

BY ARTIST

Some collectors try to acquire every comic book containing work by their favorite artist. Since some great artists have drawn literally hundreds of comic book stories, this type of collecting can be very challenging. As you come to know more and more about the style and technique of your favorite illustrator, you'll also learn more about comic book artwork in general.

BY PUBLISHER

Collectors of current superhero comics tend to be divided between "Marvel maniacs" and "DC fanatics." But there are other collectors who specialize in the comics published by smaller (sometimes extinct) companies.

BY TIME PERIOD

Certain collectors concentrate on a specific era in comic book history, often either the Golden or Silver Age. Occasionally, a collector will specialize in an even narrower time span. For example, an older collector might want to put together a collection of the comic books popular during his or her childhood. Choosing a specific decade is a good way of giving your collection an interesting historical focus.

BY GENRE

Though superhero comics have always been the most popular, every genre has its devoted collectors. People who collect according to genre usually don't limit themselves to one publisher, time period, artist, or title. Rather, they are interested in every comic book that deals with their favorite subject matter.

Back Issues

Whatever your area of interest turns out to be, you'll no longer be spending your money only on new comics. As you become a real collector, you'll also be seeking out and purchasing back issues.

Most comic book specialty shops carry a supply of recent back issues. Usually these are reasonably priced and in excellent shape (though you should never buy any comic book without inspecting it carefully from front to back). If you've been buying your new comics from one of these stores, check there first as you begin to expand your collection.

Many collectors have luck finding inexpensive back issues in places like flea markets, antique stores, used book shops, and neighborhood garage sales. You probably won't turn up many rare, old treasures, though that's always an exciting possibility. But you might come away with a real bargain.

Sooner or later, your local sources may no longer be adequate for your collecting needs. Unless you live close to a major comic book dealer or an exceptionally well-stocked specialty store, you will have to go farther afield to locate the harder-to-find issues. For serious collectors, the two major sources of back issues are mail-order dealers and comic book conventions.

Most comic books run a few advertisements from mail-order dealers. You'll be able to find many more ads in the pages of *The Official Overstreet Comic Book Price Guide* and *The Comic Buyer's Guide*. (See "For More Information," page 92.)

Pick a few dealers who seem to specialize in the kinds of comic books you collect. Send away for their catalogues or price lists. Wait until you receive them all, then check their prices against each other. When you're buying by mail, it's a good idea to comparison-shop, since prices can vary significantly. Also, always send a check or a money order instead of cash.

© 1985 DC Comics, Inc.

Keep your first order with any new dealer small. Once you've established that the dealer provides prompt, satisfactory service and that the comic books arrive in the condition you've paid for, you can begin placing other orders.

Receiving a package that contains an eagerly-awaited back issue is always an exciting experience. Even more exciting to most collectors is their first visit to a comic book convention. You can find out where and when the next major convention will be held in your area by asking with the owner of your local specialty shop or by looking in the pages of *The Comic Buyer's Guide*.

Comic book conventions are big, bustling marketplaces filled with a dazzling variety of comic books and related collectibles. In fact, they can be so dazzling that you may feel slightly overwhelmed. Before you buy anything, it's a good idea to take an unhurried tour around the entire dealer's area, checking out each person's prices and selection.

Each comic book will have its cost labelled on its protective bag. But if you're buying a number of comics from one dealer, don't be afraid to ask for a better price on the total. At conventions, most dealers expect customers to bargain and will frequently offer a significant discount. Often you can get even better buys toward the end of a convention, since many dealers would rather sell their inventory at a discount than bother to repack it and carry it back home.

Collecting versus Investing

As your collection expands, the back issues you buy are likely to become increasingly expensive. In fact, you may start to feel that you are no longer simply purchasing comic books but investing in them. Though investing and collecting are related activities, they are not identical.

To an investor, a rare comic book is a tangible asset, like a gold coin or rare painting—something to acquire, hold onto for a time, and then sell when its price has gone up. True, many comic book investors are also fans. But with the value of certain prime issues rising at such a rapid pace, more and more investors are entering the field who couldn't care less about the stories or artwork of the comics they buy.

Collectors are a different breed. The *Spider-Man* collector craves a copy of the first issue because he or she is a fan of that particular series and would love to own a complete set. The condition of the comic book may be less important than the mere fact of owning it at all. To an investor, on the other hand, buying a rare comic in the best possible condition is crucially important, since a high-quality copy is worth much more on the marketplace than the same issue in even slightly worse shape.

It is love of comics, not money, that motivates collectors. Many collectors would never think of selling their comics, no matter how much money they might get for them.

A Word About Selling

It's fun to daydream about growing rich from comic books. But it's important to be realistic. Many collectors are shocked to discover that the comics they've stored away so lovingly are worth much less than they thought.

Even prime back issues rarely get full guidebook value from dealers, who have to pay substantially less than they charge for comic books in order to make a profit. And the values of more recent comics can fluctuate wildly. A comic book that everybody wants today can lose its popularity overnight. Tomorrow, it may be worth little more than its cover price.

If you decide at some point to sell your comic books, there are three basic choices available to you. You can sell them to the owner of a specialty shop, to a dealer (this is often done at conventions), or directly to other collectors through a classified ad in a fan publication.

Each of these methods has advantages and drawbacks. Store owners and dealers are usually more interested in buying entire collections than individual issues. This is a quick and easy way of disposing of your collection and converting it into instant cash. But it is not necessarily the most profitable, since retailers and dealers pay significantly less than guidebook prices.

You can sell individual pieces of your collection for top (or close to top) dollar by advertising in a fan publication like *The Comic Buyer's Guide*. However, you must be willing to go through the trouble of placing the ad and handling the orders. In addition, there are many expenses involved, since you must pay for the ad, mailing supplies, and postage. Still, your time and investment are likely to pay off in higher profits.

CHAPTER 7

What Makes a Comic Valuable

Unlike certain other collectibles such as gold coins, comic books have little built-in value. Even if a $20 gold piece were to lose all of its interest to collectors, it would always be worth $20. By contrast, a comic book that no one cares about owning is worth nothing more than the paper it's printed on.

The value of a comic book depends entirely on demand. The more demand there is for a comic book, the more money it is worth. So what makes certain comic books more desirable to collectors than others? Let's look at some of the answers.

Characters

For reasons no one understands, some characters become very popular, while others leave fans cold. During the Golden Age, for example, readers loved the Sub-Mariner but couldn't have cared less about the Fin. Superman has been going strong since 1938. But Amazing-Man's career, which began in 1939, fizzled out less than three years later.

Though the appeal of certain characters is difficult to analyze, one thing can be said with certainty: the more popular the character, the more valuable the comic books in which he or she or it appears. For more information on the most popular characters from the Golden Age to the present, see Chapter 8.

First Issues

The first issue of a popular title is always the most valuable, largely because of its historical signifiance as the comic that launched the series. Often, though not always, a first issue also contains the original appearance of the starring character. First issues of Golden and Silver Age titles are also rare, since fewer copies of these early issues have survived.

If a title isn't popular to begin with, then the first issue won't be especially valuable. Also note that the difference in price between the first and second issues of a widely collected title can be significant. A copy of *The Incredible Hulk* #1 in near-mint conditon is valued at close to $900. By contrast, the next issue sells for slightly more than $300.

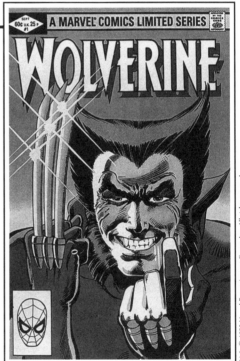

Wolverine Limited Series #1 (*September, 1982*)

Because it's so hard to predict which characters will catch on with fans, many collectors automatically buy the first issue of every new comic book that is published. If the character proves to be popular, this strategy can pay off handsomely. A first issue of Mirage Studios's *Teenage Mutant Ninja Turtles* in mint condition is already worth nearly $200, even though it is only a few years old.

Rarity

Rarity certainly contributes to the value of a comic book. But it is not the most important factor in determining how much a comic book is worth.

For example, almost all Golden Age comic books are relatively rare, since most people simply threw away their old comics in those days. Even comic books that were saved often fell apart over time. As a result, the vast majority of comic books from that period have long since disappeared.

Still, this doesn't mean that every comic book from the 1930s and 1940s is worth a great deal of money. A comic book is valuable only if other people want it for their collections and are willing to pay for it. And there are many

© 1942 DC Comics, Inc.

Wonder Woman #1 (Summer, 1942) has added value because of its age and the popular character it features.

Golden Age titles that hardly anyone collects.

Where highly sought-after comics are concerned, there is a direct relationship between rarity and value. An *Action Comics* #1 in near-mint condition is worth tens of thousands of dollars partly because there are so few available copies. The single mint-condition copy known to exist is considered priceless.

Artwork

The quality of the artwork can make a big difference in a comic book's value to collectors. An issue drawn by a popular artist is almost always worth more than a comic book illustrated by an unknown. An issue containing work by a truly major artist may be worth a significant amount of money on that basis alone.

A classic example is the first issue of *Thun'da,* a jungle adventure comic from the early 1950s. Near-mint copies of the second through the sixth issues are currently worth around $70 each. By contrast, a copy of *Thun'da* #1 in the same condition is valued at almost $700. The reason? The artwork in the first issue was done entirely by Frank Frazetta, one of the most admired and important artists in comic book history. On rare occasions, a writer's contribution enhances the value of a comic in the same way.

Milestones

Some comic books possess special value because they deal with important landmarks in the life of a character. The most significant of these issues are the ones that contain the very first appearance of a major hero. This does not always occur in a first issue. For example, Batman made his debut in *Detective Comics* #27 and Spider-Man was introduced in *Amazing Fantasy* #15.

X-Men #94 *(August, 1975) marked the beginning of the new team in its own book.*

The first appearance of an important secondary character can also give a comic book added value to collectors. *Detective Comics #37* is worth substantially more than the previous issue because it contains the first appearance of Batman's sidekick, Robin.

In the domain of superhero comics, another important

landmark is the "origin" story, which explains where a character came from and how he or she acquired special powers. Again, the origin story may or may not be the first appearance of a character.

Occasionally, an issue will take on added value because it deals with the last appearance of a character instead of the first. For example, *The Amazing Spider-Man #121* is worth five times as much

Justice League of America #29 *(August, 1964) from the popular tradition of Justice League / Justice Society cross-overs.*

as the previous issue because it depicts the death of Spider-Man's girl friend, Gwen Stacey. Similarly, the death of Robin the Boy Wonder in *Batman* #428 turned that issue into an instant collector's item.

Another occurence that generally increases the value of a comic is the "cross-over," in which a superhero guest-stars in another character's comic book. *Superman* #76, for example, contains a famous cross-over by Batman in a story called "The Mightiest Team in the World."

At other times, an issue gains value because a popular character from another comic shows up for just a few panels. This is called a "cameo."

Certain kinds of milestones apply only to a particular title. For Superman fans, *Superman* #61 has special significance because it contains the first appearance of Green Kryptonite, the only substance known to be fatal to the Man of Steel. *Fantastic Four Annual* #3 is important because it features the wedding of two of the team's members, Reed Richards and Sue Storm. *The Amazing Spider-Man* #252 is significant because Spider-Man began wearing a newly-designed costume in that issue.

Finally, certain issues are valuable because they represent milestones in the history of the comic book itself, usually major anniversaries. After the first issue, the hundredth issue is generally regarded as the most important. Subsequent centennial issues—#200, #300, and so on—are also considered special collector's items.

A new costume issue: The Amazing Spider-Man #252 *(May, 1984).*

CHAPTER 8

The Cream of the Comics

In the world of comic books, a few treasured issues are regarded as the ultimate collectibles. These rare comics are so valued that most collectors would be thrilled just to see them up close at a convention. For serious investors, they represent the "blue-chip stocks" of the comic book marketplace—proven winners whose prices have risen rapidly and show no signs of slowing down.

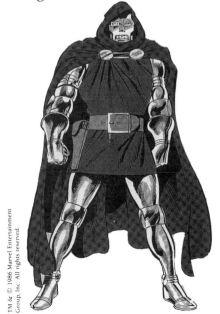

The Ten Most Valuable Comics

Superman #1

Detective Comics #27

The ten most sought-after and expensive comics in existence date from the Golden Age. The prices quoted below are for copies in Very Fine to Near Mint condition. In general, the prices of these issues have risen yearly.

1. *Action Comics* #1 (June, 1938). The first appearance of Superman, the first and greatest superhero. Value: $30,000.

2. *Marvel Comics* #1 (October/November 1939). The introduction of the Human Torch and the Sub-Mariner. Value: $27,000.

3. *Detective Comics* #27 (May, 1939). The first appearance of Batman. Value: $25,000.

4. *Superman* #1 (Summer, 1939). The first comic book created especially for an original superhero character. Value: $24,000.

5. *Whiz Comics* #1 (February, 1940). The debut appearance of Captain Marvel. Value: $18,200.

6. *Detective Comics* #1 (March, 1937). The first anthology comic devoted to single theme. Contains pre-*Superman* work by Siegel and Shuster. Value: $10,000.

7. *Batman* #1 (Spring 1940). The second comic book title to star a major superhero. Value: $9,800.

8. *More Fun Comics* #52 (February, 1940). The introduction of the ghostly Golden Age superhero, the Spectre. Value: $9,000.

9. *All American Comics* #16 (July, 1940). The origin and first appearance of Green Lantern. Value: $7,700.

10. *Captain America* #1 (March, 1941). The introduction of Simon and Kirby's Captain America. Value: $7,700.

The Ten Most Valuable Silver Age Comics

Recently, certain Silver Age comics have been appreciating at an even more dramatic rate than Golden Age rarities. The skyrocketing value of these issues has put them out of reach of the average collector. For serious investors, however, these comics are very attractive.

1. *Amazing Fantasy* #15 (August, 1962). The origin and first appearance of Spider-Man. Value: $1,800.

2. *Fantastic Four* #1 (November, 1961). The groundbreaking debut of Marvel's original superhero team. Value: $1,600.

3. *Showcase* #4 (October, 1956). Featuring a new version of the Flash, this issue marks the beginning of the Silver Age. Value: $1,600.

4. *The Amazing Spider-Man* #1 (March, 1963). With this issue, Marvel gave its most popular superhero his own magazine. Value: $1,500.

5. *Adventure Comics* #247 (April, 1958). The first appearance of the Legion of Superheroes, the popular team of 26th-century teen superheroes. Value: $1,400.

6. *Detective Comics* #225 (November, 1955). The first appearance of J'onn J'onzz, the Martian Manhunter. Value: $750.

7. *Justice League of America* #1 (October, 1960). The first issue of the series starring DC's popular superhero team. Value: $750.

8. *X-Men* #1 (September, 1963). The introduction of Marvel's team of mutant superheroes. Value: $750.

9. *The Brave and the Bold* #28 (March, 1960). The introduction of the Justice League of America. Value: $700.

10. *The Incredible Hulk* #1 (May, 1962). The origin of Marvel's green-skinned superhero. Value: $700.

X-Men #1

The Incredible
Hulk #1

Today's Hot Titles

It is difficult, if not impossible, to foresee which of today's comic books will be tomorrow's treasured back issues. The value of current comics depends on many unpredictable factors. For example, *Batman* suddenly became a red-hot seller in the wake of the 1989 hit movie. Whether collectors will still feel the same way about the Caped Crusader ten years from now is a question no one can answer with certainty.

For beginning collectors, here is an alphabetical list of some of today's fan favorites.

Spider-Man and *The Amazing Spider-Man* (Marvel). The continuing adventures of Marvel's web-slinging superhero.

Batman and *Detective Comics* (DC). The two major titles starring DC's "Dark Knight" super-detective.

Concrete (Dark Horse Comics). A beautifully written comic book about a political speechwriter who is transformed into a grotesque-looking but still deeply human creature with a massive body that seems to be made of cement.

Justice League America and *Justice League Europe* (DC). These two titles continue DC's tradition of superhero teams and feature many popular characters.

Punisher and *Punisher War Journal* (Marvel). Two titles starring Marvel's violent vigilante.

Teenage Mutant Ninja Turtles (Mirage Studios). The adventures of the strangest and most successful recent creations in comicdom: a quartet of reptilian martial artists named after Renaissance painters.

Wolverine (Marvel). Another current favorite from Marvel – a snarling mutant superhero with nasty metal claws.

X-Men and *X-Factor* (Marvel). Two titles featuring colorful gangs of heroic mutants.

CHAPTER 9

Grading, Care, and Storage

The condition of any collectible, whether it is an old stamp, a rare baseball card, or a fossilized dinosaur bone, affects its value. Generally, the better its condition, the more the object is worth.

This basic rule holds true for comic books. Newly published comics are generally in top-notch condition. Most older comics, however, show signs of wear and aging. When comic books were first invented, they were regarded as nothing more than a form of entertainment for children. For that reason, they were manufactured very cheaply – printed on inexpensive paper and bound with a couple of staples. They were not "made to last." On the contrary, they were made to be read a few times and then thrown away. Even today, when comic collecting has become such a popular hobby, the standard comic book is still manufactured out of insubstantial materials. As a result, it is particularly important to know how to judge the condition of a comic book once you begin buying back issues for your collection. Equally important is knowing how to take care of your collection so that it remains in the best possible shape.

Defects

Because of the way they are handled and the materials they are made from, comic books are subject to certain forms of wear, tear, and deterioration. To grade a comic book properly, you must be familiar with these common defects. Here is a checklist of questions to keep in mind when you are inspecting a comic book. Any of these defects will lower its condition.

THE COVER

Is the cover wrinkled, folded, creased, stained, or torn in any way? Do the edges look slightly ragged or "chipped"? Have small bits (or "flakes") of color worn away? Are there pieces missing from any of the corners? Is there writing on the cover that

doesn't belong there? Is there tape anywhere on the cover? Is the cover firmly attached to the rest of the book?

THE SPINE

Is the spine in good shape or does it curl forward? (This condition is known as "spine roll." It is generally caused by folding the pages back as the comic is being read.) Is there any splitting along the spine? Has the paper pulled away from the staples? Are the staples themselves in good condition, or have they rusted?

THE INSIDE PAGES

Are the borders of the inside pages clean and white, or have they begun to turn yellow or, even worse, brittle and brown? Are any pages missing? Is the centerfold (the sheet that forms the middle pages of the comic) loose? Has anything been scissored out of the comic book, such as a mail-order coupon? Has anyone written or crayoned on the pages? Are there major tears, stains, holes, or missing pieces?

Any of these defects will lower the condition and value of a comic book.

Grading

Grading the condition of a comic book can be a tricky business—one that sometimes boils down to a matter of personal opinion and perception. One collector's "Very Fine Minus" might be another's "Fine Plus." The difference between two grades can hinge on a defect that one person regards as minor but another views as an eyesore—a small wrinkle near the lower left-hand corner of the front cover, for example.

Fortunately for the average collector, making hairline distinctions is usually of importance only when it comes to purchasing high-grade copies of rare comics, where the difference between a "Very Fine Minus" and "Fine Plus" can mean a significant difference in monetary value. For the typical collector, familiarity with these eight major grades should be sufficient.

MINT

A perfect comic book, free of all defects – as bright and shiny as if it just rolled off the printing press.

NEAR MINT

A comic book that would be considered Mint, except for one or two extremely minor defects (such as a small speck of color missing from the cover) that keeps it from achieving absolute perfection.

VERY FINE

A comic book that shows the lightest signs of wear – perhaps a small wrinkle near one of the staples or a few small nicks on one corner. It requires a sharp eye to notice the flaws, however. At a glance, a comic book in this condition looks crisp, shiny, and almost new.

FINE

In this condition, a comic looks used, but only slightly, as if it had been read a few times by someone who handled it with great care and had then stored it away immediately. A Fine comic book might have some creases along the spine, corners that are a bit worn and rounded, or inside pages with margins that have just begun to yellow. It is still an extremely handsome comic book.

VERY GOOD

A comic that has been read and handled enough to show definite signs of wear. The shininess of the cover has faded, the corners may look a bit ragged, and the spine is usually slightly damaged. Still, there are no glaring defects such as ugly stains, major tears, or missing pieces.

GOOD

A well-worn book with a heavily creased cover, a few small tears here and there, a spine that has started to split around the staples, and inner pages that are unmistakably yellow around the edges. A comic in this condition is still acceptable-looking – but just barely.

FAIR

The best that can be said about a comic book in Fair condition is that it is complete. The cover and all the pages are present, but they are ripped, wrinkled, and heavily stained. The staples are probably rusty and the larger tears may have been repaired with tape.

POOR

A comic book in such terrible shape that it's hardly worth saving.

When it comes to grading comics, always keep in mind the old saying: You can't judge a book by its cover. Never purchase back issues without removing them from their protective bags. If you don't, you may get your newly-purchased comics home only to open the bags and discover a torn inner page or a missing mail-order coupon.

So remember: before you buy any comic, check it closely from front to back.

Care and Storage

A comic book that is not cared for properly will eventually deteriorate and fall apart. Every collector, even one with no intention of ever selling his or her comics, wants them to look as good as possible.

Some collectors buy *two* copies of a new issue, one for reading, the second for storing away in perfect, untouched-by-human-hands condition. This is fine, but it requires twice as much money. A sensible alternative is to treat your single copy as carefully as possible and then store it away

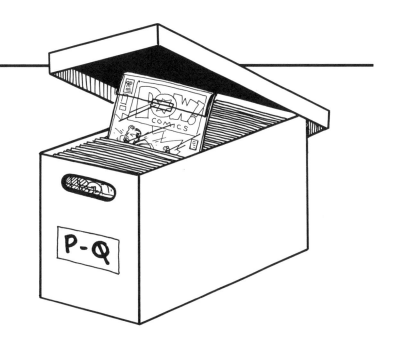

as soon as you're done reading it.

How should comics be stored? Bright light will bleach the color from a comic book, heat will turn it brown, moisture will hasten decay, and dryness will make it brittle. You should keep your collection in a place that is dark, cool, and neither too damp nor too dry. A closet in a room that's kept at a comfortable temperature and humidity level will serve nicely for the average collection.

Of course, you don't want to toss your comics into an old grocery carton at the bottom of the closet. Comics are also very fragile and can easily be torn, creased, and warped out of shape by mishandling.

Many collectors protect their comics inside storage bags. These bags are specifically manufactured to hold modern-format, Silver Age, or Golden Age issues. Some of these bags are made of inexpensive plastic and are sufficient for short-term storage (up to a year or two). Higher-quality bags are manufactured of Mylar, a superior form of plastic preferred by most serious collectors and recommended for the permanent preservation of valuable issues.

Most serious collectors also insert acid-free backing boards into the storage bags to keep their comic books from bending. Comics packaged this way can either be stacked neatly or filed upright in a specially-designed storage box made of sturdy, nonacidic cardboard.

In short, your valuable comics should be bagged, backed, and boxed. You'll have to spend a little money on storage supplies, which are available at specialty shops or from mail-order dealers, but these accessories will keep your collection in excellent shape.

Record-keeping

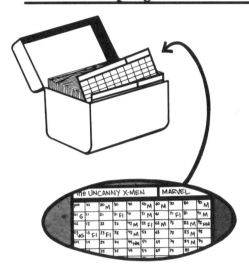

As your collection grows, you'll need some way to keep track of the comics you already own and the ones you still need.

More and more collectors are using home computers to create detailed inventories that list the titles, conditions, and purchase prices of their comics, along with other interesting information, such as the names of the featured artists.

Other collectors prefer to keep their records on index cards. These are easy to create and can be filed neatly in boxes.

Collectors seeking to collect every issue of a particular title often use loose-leaf notebooks. They list all the numbers of the title, beginning with the first issue and continuing to the current issue. Every time they acquire another issue, they check off the corresponding number on the sheet.

Whether you keep your permanent records on loose-leaf paper, file cards, or computer programs, it's a good idea to carry a separate "want list" with you. This is a piece of paper on which you record the numbers and titles of the comics you want to buy. Once your collection has reached a certain size, you'll find it hard to remember which issues you need without consulting such a list.

Glossary

Back issue Any issue of a comic book older than the one currently being sold on the stands.

Cameo A brief "guest" appearance (possibly for only a panel or two) by a character from a different comic book.

Colorist The artist who adds color to the inker's original black-and-white artwork.

Comic Code Authority The set of censoring standards adopted by the comic book industry in the 1950s. All general-distribution comics must meet these standards in order to gain the "seal of approval" from the Comics Magazine Association of America.

Convention A gathering of dealers and collectors where comic books are bought, sold, and traded. Some major conventions also feature panel discussions and guest appearances by famous comic book creators.

Crossover A major appearance (often for an entire issue) of a character from a different comic book.

Debut   The very first appearance anywhere of a comic book character.

Fanzine   A magazine about comic books published by and for fans.

Funny animal   A type of comic book featuring humorous, talking animals.

Genre   A comic book's main theme or subject matter. Examples of genres include superhero, war, western, romance, jungle, and funny animal comics.

Giveaway   A comic book given away for free, usually as an advertisement or promotion.

Golden Age   The first "heroic age" of comics, beginning with the first appearance of Superman in 1938 and lasting approximately until the end of the 1940s.

Grading   The process of judging the physical condition of a comic book.

Graphic novel   A high-quality comic book published in the form of a hardcover or large-sized paperback book.

Indicia   The publishing information that appears as a block of small type on the bottom of the first page or inside front cover of a comic book. This includes the publisher's name and address, the issue number, and legal information.

Inker   The artist who adds ink to the illustrations drawn by the penciller on the original art pages.

Letterer   The person who adds the words (dialogue, captions, and sound effects) to the original artwork.

Limited series   A comic book title that runs for a fixed number of issues, from a three-issue "mini-series" to a ten or twelve-issue "maxi-series."

Logo   The title of a comic book as it appears on the cover. Logos usually feature graphically designed words and symbols.

Origin   The story of how a person becomes a superhero and has his or her first adventure.

Original art　Large pieces of heavy paper (or "boards") containing inked, black-and-white drawings used to produce a finished comic book.

Panelology　The serious study of comics. The term was coined by comic book authority Jerry Bails, who felt that since coin collecting is called "numismatics" and stamp collecting "philately," comic collecting is entitled to a name of its own.

Penciller　The artist who draws the original illustrations for a comic book, based on a writer's storyline or script.

Reprint　A reproduction of a vintage story or comic book. An entire issue reprinted in the exact format of the original is known as a **facsimile**.

Silver Age　The great revival of superhero comics that began in the late 1950s and continued until the end of the 1960s.

Splash panel　The striking, sometimes full-page illustration that often appears on the first page of a comic book.

Writer　The person who writes the plot and then the dialogue for a comic book.

For More Information

Books

The Comic Book in America. Mike Benton. Dallas: Taylor Publishing Company, 1989.

A beautifully produced and comprehensive history, sumptuously illustrated with hundreds of full-color reproductions of rare comic book covers.

Comics: Anatomy of a Mass Medium. Reinhold Reitberger and Wolfgang Fuchs. Boston: Little Brown, 1971.

A sweeping, richly illustrated overview of comic books that surveys their history, production, artistic features, connection to mass media, and cultural significance.

Comix: A History of Comic Books in America. Les Daniels. New York: Bonanza Books, 1971.

An informative history of comic books that reprints a large number of complete stories, several in full color.

The Great Comic Book Heroes. Jules Feiffer. New York: The Dial Press, 1965.

A pioneering book about Golden Age comics written by the famous cartoonist/playwright/screenwriter. Besides Feiffer's witty, insightful comments, the book includes full-color reprints of classic Golden Age stories featuring the great superheroes of the period.

The Official Overstreet Comic Book Price Guide. Robert M. Overstreet. New York: House of Collectibles (updated annually).

This is the standard reference work that catalogues virtually every comic book ever published, along with current values for various grades. This book is packed with much additional useful information, including a list of the year's major comic conventions and hundreds of advertisements from mail order dealers. Overstreet also publishes periodic updates of its *Price Guide* which reflect up-to-date changes in the market value

of comic books. These magazine-format supplements are available at comic book specialty stores.

Ron Goulart's Great History of Comic Books. Chicago: Contemporary Books, 1986.

A lively, illustrated history of comics from the 1890s through the 1980s by one of the country's leading authorities.

The World Encyclopedia of Comics. Edited by Maurice Horn. New York: Chelsea House, 1976.

An authoritative sourcebook containing hundreds of informative entries about comics strips, comic books, and their creators.

Newspapers and Magazines

Amazing Heroes, published bi-weekly. $49.95 a year. Fantagraphic Books, 7563 Lake City Way, Seattle, Washington 98115. Tel. (206) 524–1967.

A magazine in comic book format containing news, reviews, previews, and a variety of informative columns.

The Comic Buyer's Guide, published weekly. $27.95 a year. Krause Publications, 700 E. State Street, Iola, Wisconsin 54990. Tel. (715) 445–2214.

After the *Overstreet Price Guide,* this weekly paper is the most important publication available to collectors. Besides up-to-the-minute news, reviews, and historical surveys of the field, *The Comics Buyer's Guide* is the major marketplace for dealers in back issues, original art, and storage supplies. It also runs classified ads from collectors. The newspaper is available at many shops or by subscription from the publisher.

Comics Interview, published monthly. $36 a year. Fictioneer Books Ltd., Suite 301, 234 Fifth Avenue, New York, New York 10001. Tel. (404) 782–3318.

As its title indicates, this magazine consists mostly of interviews with a wide variety of people involved in comics, from artists and writers to retailers.

The Comics Journal, published monthly. $35 a year. Fantagraphic Books, 7563 Lake City Way, Seattle, Washington 98115. Tel. (206) 524–1967.

Full of informative articles about the latest developments in the comic book world, interviews with writers and artists, and provocative essays on a wide range of comic-related topics.

Comics Scene, published bi-monthly. $15.99 a year. Starlog Communications International, Inc., 475 Park Avenue South, New York, New York 10016. Tel. (212) 689–2830.

A glossy newsstand magazine featuring articles on comic books and comic-related movies and TV shows. Many pages are in color.

Index

Pages on which illustrations appear are listed in *italics*. All comic book characters are listed under the first word of their names. You'll find additional information in the Glossary, page 87.

About the Author

Harold Schechter is a professor at Queens College who has written extensively about American popular culture. His books include Film Tricks: Special Effects in the Movies *and* Kidvid: A Parents' Guide to Children's Videos. *His involvement with comic books dates back to the 1950s, when he owned hundreds of mint condition, Golden Age superhero comics. Unfortunately, his mother threw all of them away.*